KEWI HISTORY MAGAZINE #1

MW01142300

Postcard ca. 1918 – Image courtesy of *Copper World* - 101 Fifth Street

PREVIOUSLY TITLED CALUMET HISTORY MAGAZINE

Keweenaw History Magazine © 2011, 2018 Richard Buchko dba Calumet History and Hobby. Published at 109 Fifth Street #5, Calumet MI 49913. All photos taken by the author unless otherwise indicated or in the public domain. Some articles contained herein are in the public domain; for those not in public domain, all rights are reserved.

WELCOME TO KEWEENAW HISTORY MAGAZINE

ORIGINAL INTRODUCTION TO CALUMET HISTORY MAGAZINE

It is often said that every place is the same in that every place is different. I was born and raised in a town that was, to me, unique and interesting. Most people have pride in their town, whether born there or adopting it sometime in life. What makes Calumet worthy of its own magazine? Simply that the rich history of Calumet, like much of the Keweenaw, is complex, covering hundreds of years, and will never fully be told. The modern history of Calumet, which officially began with the founding of Red Jacket a century and a half ago, is ongoing. It's still here, and through its ups and downs has remained a place apart. Nestled in the middle of some of the most beautiful land in the world, facing some of the least hospitable weather, it had its day as a powerhouse of industry while at the same time tucked away in a corner of the country, and settled by one of the most diverse populations the country has ever known, Calumet can lay claim to uniqueness above and beyond just being *a little different*. If you need further proof, simply look at how many books have been written about Calumet and the Keweenaw. Few cities can boast as many different perspectives of the past, present, and future as the towns of the Keweenaw, because for all the good and the bad of the last couple hundred years, it's something people here still care about.

Calumet History Magazine will offer an ongoing look at the past, the present, and ultimately the future of Calumet. Anyone with a story to tell is invited to take part. Past histories will be studied, debated, and where necessary refuted. New ideas will emerge, and new points of view will be uncovered. Each issue will stand alone, but over the course of time it is hoped that Calumet History Magazine will be an accumulated chronicle of this town and the surrounding area. Where it will go depends on the readers – what they want, what they offer, what they care about.

What do you have to share? Your stories, opinions, photos, and ideas will make up the future issues. Don't be shy.

Rich Buchko
Editor/Publisher

ARE *YOU* GOOD FOR THE ECONOMY?

Have you considered if you are good the the economy of Calumet? Yes, *you* – are you helping or hurting the economy in town? All of us make money, and all of us spend money. Where we make it and where we spend it can be thought of like a balance sheet, and in the end we are either bringing money into town and helping the economy, or we're sending money out of town and hurting it.

Where we make our money is something over which we have limited control. I am a writer; I sell books and I complete projects for clients. Although I sell books locally, most of my income is from other cities and others states. Through writing clients or books I sell online, in that sense I am bringing money into town, much the way a tourist who visits Calumet leaves money behind at the shops, hotels and restaurants. Some of us are paid by local companies, some by regional or national companies, or by governmental programs. Whatever the method or source, we're all bringing money into town.

The important factor, though, isn't how we get it, but where we spend it. If we spend money locally, it helps the economy of the area, and the closer we spend it to home, the more it is likely to help here. We're all looking for a bargain, that's natural, but sometimes we hurt ourselves tomorrow by trying to save a little money today. If I am looking for a book, and I can find it locally for $5, that's $5 that I've put back into the economy of the area. If I find it online for $4 and buy it, yes, I have saved a dollar, but where is all that money going? – *out of town*. It's tempting to subscribe to a DVD-delivery service online instead of visiting the local video store, but if you're paying $20/month you are sending $240/year out of town. Is it worth driving down the street to keep a few hundred dollars in Calumet? I think so – plus, when Sherri at Superior Video makes a recommendation for a movie it's a lot more fun to complain about her opinion in person.

If I need a widget that I can find at the local hardware store, I might be tempted to order it online for less or travel down to Houghton and get it at WalMart. No one would blame me if I saved a few dollars. But might it be worth a dollar here and there to keep the money in town? Money spent in Calumet is likely to stay in Calumet. The money I spent on the widget is delivered to an employee in wages, who spends it at a local shop for a gift. That money is placed in the local bank, where it is part of a loan to a resident putting in new windows. The money is paid to a local installer, who has dinner that night at a local restaurant..... that same dollar is used over-and-over again. If I order it online, I send the money out of town, and that's it – the money is not here to be used over and over; it hurts Calumet.

If I can spend it in Calumet, that's the best place. Calumet is not a big city, though; we cannot find everything we need here. If I can't get it here, and I spend it in Houghton instead, at least the money is being spent nearby. If I can spend it at a locally-owned Houghton store instead of a corporate chain, so much the better, because the money is more likely to be used over-and-over in town that way instead of paying for offices in Chicago. If I can't find what I need in Houghton, then Marquette is the next best choice – it's not local, but at least it's U.P. If I have to spend it elsewhere, looking for a Michigan company is the next best option – again, at least it's helping the state rather than Arkansas.

How much of your money are you spending locally? How much is going to Houghton, to Marquette, to Michigan.... or to China? The phrase "Buy American" is often used, but where it is made is nowadays less important than where it is sold. It helps the local economy more if you buy something made in China from the corner shop, than if you by an American product from Salt Lake City.

Of course, I am not suggesting that you refuse to save a lot of money in order to buy locally. Sometimes, even if we can find what we need or want here, it's more expensive, and we have bills and budgets to worry about. Even a few dollars here and there can matter. But if you look through this magazine you'll find shops and businesses with many products and services to offer; at least check out the service, quality, and price before turning away from town. Consider your time and effort. I can get my six-pack of low-sodium V-8 for $4.12 at WalMart, and it costs $4.99 in town; sure, I'd love to save $.87, but isn't it worth about 15-cents a can to be able to get it down the street, and to keep the money in town?

Before sending your money away, consider what you have in Calumet, and how important it is to keep businesses going. Then, try the rest of the Keweenaw if you must, then the U.P., then the state. The closer to home you spend your money, the better it is for you, for me, and for all of us. It keeps businesses going, prices down, and helps make sure that Calumet can grow.

So..... are you good for the economy?

ARE YOU TRYING TO FOOL ME?
IN CALUMET, MICH.

Did you realize Calumet was such an amorous town?

These 1915 postcards suggest that mining, logging and hunting were not the only treasures being sought.

Okay – we know these are not pictures of Calumet and the name of the town was simply stamped onto a commercial postcard, but if you close your eyes and use your imagination, is it so hard to envision?

HOPE YOU ENJOYED YOURSELF
IN CALUMET, MICH.

Send your images of days gone by, and be a part of a future issues of Calumet History Magazine.

All images will be scanned and immediately returned to the owner.

Rich Buchko
Calumet History and Hobby
109 Fifth Street #5
Calumet MI 49913
historyandhobby@yahoo.com

THE TOLEDO WAR
or How Calumet Ended Up in Michigan

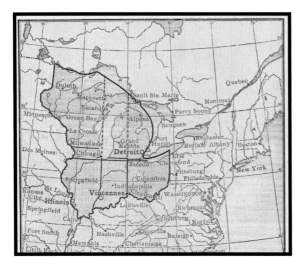

THE NORTHWEST TERRITORY – Map from Dodge's Advanced Geography, Michigan Edition – 1910

It's not something typically taught in Michigan schools: the time we went to war (almost) with Ohio; the year we fought for Toledo and only grudgingly accepted the Upper Peninsula instead.

The Northwest Ordinance of 1787 was the first step taken by the United States to create new states out of the land not already part of the existing states. The Northwest Territory incorporated what became the modern states of Ohio, Michigan, Indiana, Illinois, and Wisconsin. Once a territory had a population of 60,000 (free adult males) they could form a state government, adopt a constitution and apply for admission into the Union. The first to gain admission was Ohio, in 1803.

In the 1830's, as Michigan began forming its state government and applied for admission, a conflict with Ohio led to what came to be known as *The Toledo War* (also called by some as *The Michigan-Ohio War* or *The Bloodless War*).

The argument brewed over a small strip of land along the Michigan-Ohio border, called the Toledo Strip. When the Northwest Ordinance was passed in 1787 Michigan's southern boundary was designated as a line drawn from the southern tip of Lake Michigan due east to where it meets Lake Erie. Unfortunately, the location of the southern tip of Lake Michigan was incorrectly calculated because maps in those early days were largely inaccurate. In 1818 a survey discovered the true boundary line, but Ohio, the existing state, already claimed the Toledo Strip. When Michigan formed a government and applied for statehood, she wanted her Ordinance-designated boundaries, including the strip of land which included the Port of Toledo – considered a very important city as a future shipping port. Ohio refused, and even blocked Michigan's admittance into the Union.

Michigan and Ohio both feverishly claimed the Toledo Strip, and passed laws making it a crime for anyone to obey the laws of the other state.

Both states had valid arguments: Ohio was already a Constitutionally-admitted state and had claimed the Toledo Strip for decades, while Michigan had the letter of the Northwest Ordinance; Ohio claimed that the Northwest Ordinance had been superseded by the Constitution and was no longer valid, while Michigan had the support of the U.S. Attorney General who backed up its claim; Ohio stated that Congress accepted her borders by admitting the state to the Union, but Michigan pointed out that the changes to Ohio's borders were not specifically acted on in Congress, and that

Ohio merely inferred acceptance; Ohio had claimed the Toledo Strip for years, but Michigan actually possessed and governed it.

Militias were formed, and two armies even marched toward one another to battle for the right to this small parcel land. It appeared that for the first time the United States would have a civil war.

One man was arrested by Michigan authorities: Major Ben Stickley of the Ohio Militia. One man was injured: Sheriff Joseph Wood was stabbed in the thigh by Major Stickley's son. No armies fought, however: The two enemy legions each were stuck in a swamp and failed to locate one another, and then cooler heads prevailed.

Congress was split on who should receive the disputed land, and joint governance was called for until a settlement could be negotiated. Ohio agreed, but Michigan refused, believing that any compromise would weaken its claim. In 1836 a settlement was finally reached – forced on Michigan as a condition of finally being admitted as a state. Ohio would retain the Toledo Strip, and as compensation Michigan would receive three-fourths of the land to the north known as the Upper Peninsula. Michigan was furious to be forced to accept this remote and commercially worthless piece of land in exchange for a thriving commercial port. However, not long after, when the true mineral resources of the Upper Peninsula – especially the copper of the Keweenaw – were realized, Michigan finally felt she received the good part of the deal.

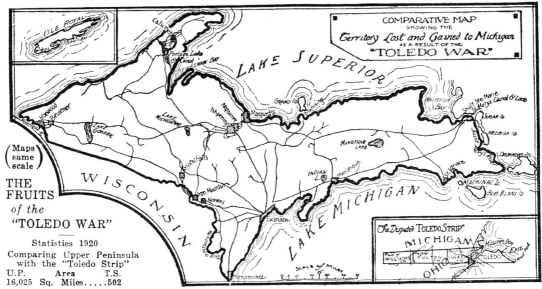

THE RELATIVE SIZES OF WHAT OHIO RECEIVED AND MICHIGAN WAS "FORCED" TO ACCEPT. It is universally understood that Michigan got the better deal, though at the time Michigan felt cheated. From *The Story of Michigan* **by Claude Larzelere – 1929**

Where to find out more:

The Toledo War by Don Faber.
University of Michigan Press - 2008

FIRST HAND COMMENTS ON THE TOLEDO WAR

> In 1824, at the age of seven, R. C. Crawford traveled from Ontario to the territory of Michigan. In 1881 he shared some of his early memories, which by fortune happened to include his short stint in the Michigan militia during the Toledo War – a war that it seems even the soldiers had difficulty taking seriously.
>
> --- R. Buchko

(From "Reminiscences of Pioneer Life in Michigan" by Rev. R. C. Crawford of Michigan Conference of the Methodist Episcopal Church. *Michigan Pioneer Historical Collections Vol. 4 – 1883*)

In those days all able-bodied males between the ages of eighteen and forty-five years were required to perform military duty, and all such had their names enrolled, and were required twice a year to spend one day in hard military drill, not knowing how soon our knowledge of military tactics might be of great service to our country; and there soon came a time when we found it out, for in the summer of 1835 our little Michigan had some "unpleasantness" with her big sister Ohio, which resulted in a fearful war, and the destruction of many lives of chickens and honey bees, and occasionally a turkey. Being myself of a military turn of mind and fond of excitement, I cheerfully obeyed my country's call and started out "with humble knapsack on my back," "a poor but honest soldier," and as I did all my military drilling and must do all my fighting with my little boxwood fife, I therefore went forth playing cheerfully, *The Girl I Left Behind Me.* Our march lasted the best part of four days, traveling most of the time at good speed, and occasionally sitting down to a lunch of fresh chicken and a bunch of well filled honey-comb, brought in by some foraging party who had been straggling off in search of some fresh water to drink and on a skirmishing expedition. But what grieved us most of all was the fact that after marching all the way to the banks of the Maumee, we found Governor Lucas had stayed away with all of his forces, and left us to do our fighting with the only man we could find, who was ready for the fight, and he preferred sending out his pigs and chickens to the slaughter rather than to come out himself.

We spent two nights and one whole day in drill, under the leadership of General Brown, of precious memory, showing the Buckeyes what Michigan troops could do in the matter of fight, if they could find a "foe worthy of their steel." Satisfied with our achievements and glorious victories, our worthy "Commander in chief," our "Boy Governor," as we all called him, Stevens T. Mason, ordered "a right about face," "shoulder arms," and a "forward march, homeward," which we were all, by this time, quite ready to obey. So we were soon formed in line, and our martial band struck up the "Soldier's Return," and as we thought of "home, sweet home," and the "girls we left behind us," we were soon moving off in rapid march, disgusted enough with war, and fully resolved "we would beat our swords into ploughshares," and our "spears into pruning hooks," and never "learn war any more." We were soon home, and our weapons of warfare were laid aside, and we were all soon regarded as citizens again, instead of being looked upon as bloodthirsty soldiers, as they considered us a few days before.

> In reality *The Toledo War*, had shots ever been exchanged in earnest, could have become a terrible chapter in United States history. While it is possible to poke fun after the fact, real armies with loaded guns planned to protect their "rights" (as they each saw them), and it was a combination of luck and finally a little common sense that saved the day.
>
> --- R. Buchko

Excerpt from the poem "Lake Superior"

by Will J. Massingham, published in *Lake Superior & Other Poems* – 1904)

Cites and homes are but man's sign
Where himself can clothe and sleep and dine.
Their grandeur comes form Mother Earth,
Who gave all men and things their birth.
And grand some are and hence we hie
To where two others strangely lie.
Though true to thought of other towns,
Duluth the crown of commerce crowns,
We'll stay, we'll stay upon the way,
Nor hasten on for many a day,
But view the wonders of the rounds,
Sequestered here in hidden vale,
These towns reveal a charming tale.
They do not lie, they do not stand,
They cling, for there is naught of level land.
To strange canals we'll sail away,
Land-locked with Linden's two canals
Are Hancock, Houghton, Dollar Bay.
Here cross on promontory free,
Extending far into the sea -
('Tis Keweenaw, soft Indian name,
That gave this copper world-wide fame)
Here nature sank a furrow deep
And left rich hillsides, fine and steep -
These waters strange are deep, not wide
And coppers tinge has stained their pride.
(Did copper make poor Indian brown,
As copper made this double town?)
Here lovers toss a noonday kiss
Across this natures kind abyss,
And when its silent tide congeals
Across the ice not far he steals.
Why can't the boys with bat and ball
Play o'er such chasm, long, deep, but small?
And surely friend with friend here lives,
Where contact close sweet nature gives.
These do not stand, but safely cling,
Like mighty stone in giant's sling,

To each hillside
        Where'er betide
        This unique pride.
And here's that school, the school of mines,
Amid these wondrous mines and pines -
A school that teaches many a thing,
While widening blessings from it spring
        Benign, worldwide!
Here rolls brown copper's tidal wave
Adown those slopes from Calumet -
Electric wizard's worldwide slave.
Who sees this hidden world unique
Another such will vainly seek.
Rich, soundless mines miles, miles extend
And 'neath the lake they fail to end.
And when we think 'twill ever last,
And scan the wonders of its past,
The human mind that skillful weaves
These brown and ductile copper threads
Wherever thoughtful action spreads,
We wonder well and stand aghast!
Who can set its uses bounds
Or limit all its future's rounds?
As once it crowned the savage brow
So now it guides electric motions,
Climbs all Earth's heights and 'neath Earth's oceans,
Transmits the tones of social man.
Thy hillsides' greenness, thy toiling one, above, beneath the ground,
We bid adieu to roam again Superior's round.
Adieu, adieu, dear towns, to you,
These sister towns are good and rare,
I will not find their like elsewhere.

DID YOU KNOW....?

Calumet has 11 places registered with the State Of Michigan as historic sites – more than any other town in Houghton County!

Welcome to the town of Hulbert, Michigan?

by Richard Buchko

What we know today as Calumet was in the years just before the civil war nothing but forest. Copper mining had been occurring in the Keweenaw for many years, but the land in the middle of the peninsula had only been slightly explored. In 1858 Edwin J. Hulbert was surveying for a future road when he discovered some copper imbedded in rocks in the wooded areas where Calumet sits today. He found enough evidence to convince him that a substantial lode of copper existed in the area. Hulbert buried what he had found, and it wasn't until six years later, in 1864, that a barrel of the rock was shipped to Boston to convince businessmen in the area that there was likely a lode of copper waiting to be mined. The *Calumet Mining Company* and the *Hecla Mining Company* were formed.

Hulbert himself was replaced in 1866 by Alexander Agassiz, who for the next four decades developed and operated the Calumet & Helca mines, and is responsible in large part for the Calumet we know today. Hulbert was known as a skilled engineer and cartogrpaher, though his business management was suspect and he never achieved the financial success he sought. Still, credit should be given to Edwin J. Hulbert – the man who discovered the riches of Calumet.

Calumet for many years was not a town at all, but simply a place, a mine location. Villages and mine locations sprang up all around – Blue Jacket, Red Jacket Shaft, Albion, Raymbaultown, and others. The mine shafts and surrounding areas of Calumet Mine, Hecla, and South Hecla were generally referred together as Calumet, but as the area grew that name spread to cover much of the area. Red Jacket, Hecla, Laurium, and the other locations all fell under the unbrella name for the area of Calumet.

The area grew quickly. The village of Red Jacket – modern day Calumet – was platted in the late 1860's. Interestingly, Sixth Street was planned as the main street of the town, with Fifth Street intended as an alleyway.

Towns evolved and changed, and with them their names. In 1895 the village of Calumet adopted the name Laurium, and by 1910 (according to a geography book of that time which sits in my library), the village of Red Jacket was known as Calumet, although that name change didn't officially take place until many years later.

Hulbert died in 1910, always believing he had never been given full credit for his accomplishments. Perhaps that is true – he is seldom spoken of as the founder of Calumet, an honor which he deserves.

The next issue of Calumet History Magazine will contain an in-depth look at the naming of locations and towns, and how they changed over the years. If you have any information regarding this subject, please contact me.

THIS 1910 MAP SHOWS THE TOWNS OF THE KEWEENAW NOT MUCH DIFFERENT THAN THEY ARE TODAY.

MYTHS AND LEGENDS

(Reprinted from
The Keweenaw Puzzle
by Richard Buchko - 2008)

Legends are interesting; legends are often fun.

Legends sometimes are based on cold, hard fact, and completely true. Other times they are closer to the truth, to varying degrees. Occasionally they are pure fabrication, a rumor started accidentally or intentionally, something that got out of hand.

The Flying Dutchman, The Fountain of Youth, George Washington and the Cherry Tree – these and countless other stories are part of our mythos. Though many are obvious fantasy, when just realistic enough they are sometimes blended with true history, passed on from generation to generation and accepted as fact. In the movie *The Man Who Shot Liberty Valance* a reporter declined to print the truth saying, "When the legend becomes fact, print the legend." This happens more often than most people think.

The Keweenaw has a rich and exciting history. Whether you're a native of the peninsula or one of the many transplants who came to love it, you've no doubt heard stories of the past. Most are true – some are not. With a history as interesting as we have, do we need false legends? I believe that the truth is enough – and more often than not, the truth is as fascinating, or even more so, than any colorful-but-untrue stories.

CALUMET WAS ALMOST THE CAPITAL OF MICHIGAN AND LOST TO LANSING BY ONLY ONE VOTE?

The capital of a state is an important designation for any town, offering economic advantages, historical significance, and a great measure of pride. During its heyday Calumet had a large population - over 25,000 in Calumet Township at its peak[1] and close to 5,000 in Red Jacket (modern day Calumet) - plus the Keweenaw held close to 100,000 people. It was one of the largest industrial centers in the state, and quickly took advantage of social and technological innovations as they became available, at one time producing over half the copper mined in the USA. It truly was a city worthy of consideration as a state capital.

Unfortunately, that all happened about a half century too late, and hundreds of miles too far north.

The capital of Michigan had been Detroit since the state was formed in 1837, but because of its proximity to Canada, Detroit was considered vulnerable to attack by the British; so it had been known for years that a new capital would be voted and founded in 1847. In addition, the western portions of the state were beginning to develop, so a location accessible to Lake Michigan was desired.

In 1847 Calumet Township had roughly 1,200 residents and was little-known to anyone outside the Upper Peninsula. The copper boom was still about 20 years away; the Keweenaw was a largely inaccessible strip of frontier tucked away in the mostly-ignored land of the U.P. Is it possible that someone in the legislature proposed making it the state capital? Sure, a representative of the Keweenaw could have suggested it, but the idea would never have been considered because:

- The area was mostly wilderness, without much commercial impact.
- The U.P. wasn't even considered by many lower Michigan residents as a proper part of the state. The U.P. had been accepted as a consolation prize for giving up the Toledo port to Ohio in the 1830's.
- It was critical to locate a capital centrally in the state, because travel in those days was much more difficult – a hundred miles meant days of travel. To place a capital 600 miles from the most populous city, and put it where it couldn't be reached for months on end in the winter, would have been unthinkable.

Ann Arbor, Grand Rapids, Jackson, and Marshall all vied for the honor, but the lawmakers charged with reaching a decision couldn't agree on one city over another. Finally, they compromised on a place north of Ann Arbor, east of Grand Rapids, and West of Jackson and Detroit: a largely unsettled township called Lansing. The House voted 48-17 in favor of Lansing, and the Senate voted 12-8 to seat it there. Calumet – or anyplace in the Keweenaw – was never part of the picture.

By the time the Keweenaw became populous and commercially important, Lansing had already been the capital for many years, and the permanent Capitol building had been erected. Even at the turn of the century, if some enterprising Keweenaw representative had proposed a change in the capital in recognition of the importance of Copper Country, because of the winters and the travel it not only wouldn't have "lost by one vote," it would have not been seriously considered.

In local books and online you find many statements such as, "I've heard that Calumet was even considered for the state capital," "… known famously as the runner up in the decision…having lost to Lansing by only one vote," and "lost the vote for state capital by only one vote." Where the story started or how it got so readily accepted I can't say, but for all its significance to Michigan and its glory in history, Calumet was never considered.

In 1875, at a meeting of the Pioneer Society of Michigan, Levi Bishop gave a speech in which he recounted the removal of the capital from Detroit to Lansing. He suggested that it was first presented as a joke, and voted on by the House of Representatives as a joke, only taken seriously when the bill was passed to the Michigan Senate. There a huge debate raged as one Senator complained of Lansing:

"Shall we take the capital(sic) from a large and beautiful city [Detroit], where there are ample accommodations, and stick it down in the woods and the mud on the banks of Grand River, amid choking miasma, - where even the woodman's ax has never awakened its echoes, where the howls of wolves, where the hissing of massasaugas[2] and the groans of bull-frogs resound to the hammer of the woodpecker and the solitary notes of the nightingale?

"Such were the efforts made and arguments used to defeat what was started as a good joke, but was now denounced not only as a great mistake, but as a great iniquity, and even a gigantic fraud and swindle. The members from Wayne county, who voted for the joke now hung their heads in sorrow and mortification, while nothing could arrest the onward march of legislation. The bill passed the Senate without amendment, it was immediately sent to the Governor, who at once signed it, and thus gave it the force of law."

This is the only account I discovered that suggests the compromise which resulted in Lansing winning the prize was started as a joke, one which got out of hand. While this account was offered only 28 years after the event, by someone who was allegedly there, I wonder if this, too, is a false legend which simply got carried forward.

[1] Inflated estimates of the population of Calumet Township are common – from 40,000 to as much as 100,000 – but the total in Calumet Township never topped more than 30,000.

[2] Snakes.

STOP IN AND FIND SOME LONG-LOST RELATIVES

Are you researching some family history? Looking for a long-lost grandparent? One service offered at *Copper World* (101 Fifth Street) is a chance to look through their county directories from 1989, 1903, and 1930.

"I've seen people literally break down in tears," said Tony of *Copper World*. "They spent their entire lives not knowing where great-grandma came from or where she lived, only to discover her in one of these books." The directories are well-worn and the pages browning, but that just adds to the value.

Along with the names and addresses of all the residents and businesses throughout Houghton county, the ads which occupy every page are histories in themselves. If it wasn't for the thousands of beautiful and important items you'll find at Copper World, a person could spend all day just flipping through these pages of a century ago.

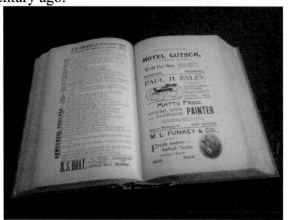

FAMILY PHOTOS

(Reprinted from *The Second Keweenaw Reader*, 2011)

THE CAR SHOULD GIVE A CLUE, AS SHOULD THE DRESS

CHRISTMASTIME – WHEN? WHERE? WHO? VERY INTERESTING RUGS. Edith? Idith? (At bottom)

AT THE LAKE SUPERIOR SHORE

This small collection of original photos was found in a Calumet shop. It struck me that this is/was someone's family, and almost certainly today's family would not have these photos, because these are apparently originals. I am certain these are Keweenaw-area photos, so maybe – just maybe – someone will recognize this family and be able to shed some light on their story.

ONE BIG (REASONABLY) HAPPY FAMILY

It's possible that someone today will recognize someone from yesterday. One woman appears in four of the photos – can she be identified?

Let's solve this mystery together!

VISIT
COPPER WORLD
101 Fifth Street
Calumet MI 49913

WHAT DOES IT MEAN?

Calumet: A *calumet* is a long-stemmed ceremonial pipe used by many native American tribes. It is usually highly-decorated, and the first known use in the European languages was in 1698. It was typically used to signify peace between friends, and has often been referred to as the "peace pipe." The word *calumet*, because of the connection with peace, has also been used to indicate a place of calm and serenity.

Hecla: The original Hecla mine was named after an Icelandic volcano, which has had over a dozen major eruptions in the last 800 years, including on in 1970. It is thought by some to be the gate to purgatory. Honestly, I'm not sure I would have used that for the name of my deep underground mine. I'm not superstitious, but why tempt fate...?

Ahmeek: This name is derived from the Ojibwa word *amik*, which means beaver. Ahmeek village is the only incorporated municipality in in Keweenaw County, which makes it the largest incorporated city in the largest county in the largest state east of the Mississippi. Wow – not bad for a town with fewer than 200 people named after a beaver!

CALUMETANIA

The Keweenaw can lay claim to a number of superlatives, such as the first professional hockey champions (The Portage Lake Pioneers in 1904) and perhaps the oldest commercial mining in North America, to name just a couple. Calumet has its share of claims to fame and unusual events:

MICHIGAN"S OLDEST CONCRETE PAVEMENT – A section of Portland Street contains this stretch of road, now over a century old. I guarantee you it's in better shape than most of the roads built in the last decade! Some sources claim that Woodward Avenue in Detroit was first, but that wasn't paved until 1909.

MICHIGAN'S OLDEST FAMILY-OWNED JEWELRY STORE: Herman Jewelers at 220 Fifth Street was founded by Joseph Hermann in 1864, and moved to Calumet in 1868. Read the full story elsewhere in this magazine.

WHEN THOMAS JEFFERSON LAID OUT HIS PLAN FOR THE FUTURE STATES OF AMERICA, CALUMET WAS IN THE LAND KNOWN AS "SYLVANIA": Although Congress accepted Jefferson's plan, they didn't record the names, which left that open for future politicians to decide.

CALUMET AND MOST OF THE UPPER PENINSULA AS PART OF THOMAS JEFFERSON'S "SYLVANIA."

IN 1910 RED JACKET SPENT OVER $1,200 ON THE 4TH OF JULY CELEBRATION - In 2010 dollars, that's about $28,000!

ONE OF THOSE STORIES THAT MAKE YOU LAUGH, BUT SHOULDN'T – Local Newspapers in April 1902 tell the story of "an insane Finnish woman" who left her bed in the middle of a cold spring night, walked out to the barn, and for reasons unknown (except maybe that insanity thing) strangled a large calf.

Herman Jewelers
Michigan's Oldest Family-Operated Jewelry Store
A Family and Calumet Tradition for Almost 150 Years

Two words that are easy to get used to when talking about Calumet are first and oldest. Herman Jewelers, which for the last 47 years has been located at the corner of Sixth and Oak Streets, can lay claim to both, starting with being the oldest family owned jewelry store in Michigan. For almost 150 years Herman Jewelers has served Calumet and the Keweenaw.

In 1863 Joseph Hermann left Germany to make his way in the frontier land of the Upper Peninsula. It took a tremendous amount of courage to emigrate to land full of

JOS. HERMAN AND FAMILY - 1870'S

opportunities but with no guarantees, and a country in the middle of a Civil War, but Joseph Hermann not only survived, he thrived. He opened his jewelry shop in the Cliff Mine area of the Keweenaw in 1864. When he moved to Calumet in 1868 with his family, buying the first deeded lot in the village of Red Jacket, he couldn't know that he would be starting a family tradition that would last well into the 21st Century.

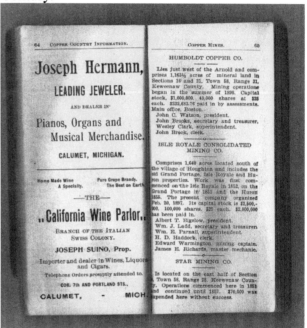

LOCAL DIRECTORY – 1895

The business would occupy a number of buildings in Calumet, and five generations of the Hermann/Labonte families later, Edward Labonte, Joseph's great-great-grandson continues this tradition of service. Ed has been part of the family business since 1973, and the owner since he bought the business from his father, Herman Labonte, in 1984.

The Herman Jewelers family has seen, and been a part of, a lot of history in Calumet. Edward's great-grandfather, John "Foxy" Hermann was the first business-owner in Calumet to heat his building with steam, and one of the first to experience the new telephone, and electrical service. He was there when the

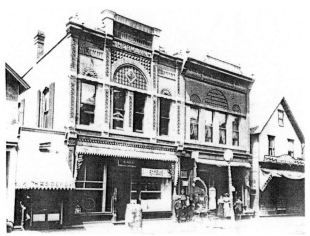

**HISTORICAL PHOTO OF
HERMANN BUILDING**

first newspaper in the town, Red Jacket News, starting publishing in 1889. In the early days of Herman Jewelers people could fish on Elm Street, dropping their lines between the planks of the wooden sidewalk. Herman Jewelers saw the village grow with the copper boom of the late 19th and early 20th centuries, with much of the construction funded by licensing fees from the 86 different saloons in town.

Today, Edward Labonte continues a family tradition and a Calumet tradition, adding another proud list of first, oldest, and best to the history of this area.

Calumet Photos - Do you Recognize Anyone?

**HERMAN JEWELERS - TODAY
220 FIFTH STREET**

CALUMET, HECLA & RED JACKET – 1881

It may seem hard to believe that only a dozen years before this remarkably accurate illustration was made, Calumet was nothing more than a few small shops and houses lost in the woods near a mine shaft, newly begun. The population was no more than 300, if that.

Seen here are the villages of Red Jacket on the left, Calumet (now Laurium) on the right, and surrounding locations. In 1880 Red Jacket itself had over 2,100 people, and would peak at close to 5,000 around the time of the 1913 strike. Fewer than 1,000 lived in Calumet (Laurium), which by the time of the strike had swelled to over 8,000 resident. Many of the homes and other buildings in the illustrations are still standing and can be identified.

The large clearing, part of which is now Agassiz Park, was used as a community pasture for the grazing of cattle and other common needs.

Calumet has an elevation of over 1200 feet, and the township now rests on over 2,000 miles of water-filled mine shafts.

HOUSING IN THE MICHIGAN COPPER DISTRICT AT THE TIME OF THE 1913 STRIKE

(From *Strike Investigation* by The Committee of the Copper Country Commercial Club of Michigan – 1913)

During the infamous strike of 1913 rumors and misinformation were rampant – on both sides of the issue. A group of about 500 business leaders, who formed the Copper Country Commercial Club (something like a Chamber of Commerce today) decided to investigate the conditions, issues, and activities surrounding the strike, in the hopes of providing an objective set of facts which might lead to a quicker and better solution. Certainly you can imagine that the drastic reduction of income among miners and the company had a profound impact on the businesses of the city, so it was in their best interests to see it end, quickly.

One area of information which had likely never been studied before, was the housing of the miners. As of July 1913 there were some 14,300 miners working in the Copper Country, and they all needed to live somewhere. The situation described by the Copper Country Commercial Club suggests that of the many issues causing trouble between the miners and the companies, housing was not one of them. In most cases the rent being paid was less than two days wages out of a month – a condition many of us would love to share today.

--- R. Buchko

In the Michigan Copper District, as in most other mining camps, whenever a company begins to operate, one of the problems is the housing of the men, in most cases the mine being located some distance away from any village or city. It has been the policy of the mining companies operating in the Michigan Copper District to build whatever houses were necessary upon their own land and to lease or rent the houses to their employees. In no case is an employee compelled to live in a company house – on the contrary, because of the very moderate rents that are charged in the Copper Country, company houses are in such great demand that the mining companies have a great many applications for each house. On account of the severity of the winters in the Lake Superior District, houses are built substantially and with a view toward comfort in extremely cold weather. They type of houses, the rent charged, and the accommodations afforded to the tenants are about the same in all the mining locations. In the early days of the mining industry many of the houses built were log houses, a few of which may still be seen in the various mining locations. Of late years the log houses have gradually disappeared and have been replaced by frame dwelling houses, similar to those in the photographs. In some instances, where the company has not a sufficient number of houses to accommodate all of its employees and in some instances where employees have desired to own their own homes, the companies have rented lots to employees who have built there own houses thereon.

In the next column is a table showing the number of houses owned by employees paying ground rent to the company, the usual size of the lots and the annual ground rent for the various companies:

RENTS

The following is some data with reference to each company as to the houses rented, the size, the rents charged, and the improvements and accommodations to tenants:

The Mohawk Mining Company rents 53 single-frame houses with 5 and 6 rooms and a barn, for $5.50 per month. It rents 63 double-frame houses with ten rooms and a barn for $5.50 for each side of the house. Water is supplied to the location by wells.

LOTS RENTED TO MINE WORKERS

Mining Company	No. of Houses	Lot Size	Yearly Rent
Mowhawk	120	100x125	$6.00
Ahmeek	0	---	---
Allouez	15	75x100	$5.00
Osceola	81	50x100	$5.00
Wolverine	64	100x100	$6-10.00
Centennial	27	75x100	$5.00
Calumet & Hecla	~1000	60x120	$5.00
Tamarack	30	5300 sq.	$5.00
LaSalle	0	---	---
Laurium	0	---	---
Franklin	30	50x125	$5.00
Oneco	0	---	---
Quincy	202	50x100/ up	$5.00
Hancock Consolidated	2	50x100	$5.00
Isle Royale	0	---	---
The Superior	0	---	---
Copper Range	144	50x100	$5.00
		75x100	$6.00
Winona	36	50x100	$1.00
Approximate Total	~1751		$1-10/yr.

The Ahmeek Mining Company has

    7 - 4 room frame dwelling houses at $4.00 per month
    2 - 4 room frame dwelling houses at $3.50 per month
   20 - 5 room frame dwelling houses at $5.00 per month
    1 – 7 room frame dwelling houses at $4.00 per month
   28 - 7 room frame dwelling houses at $6.00 per month

Each house has a 12 x 12 barn. There is no water system under pressure but most of the families have piped water from wells to force pumps in their kitchens. The company charges five cents per kilowatt per hour for electric light, and the rent includes the removal of garbage whenever necessary. The company has supplied its employees with fuel, when requested, at the following prices: Pittsburgh soft coal in lump, delivered to house, five dollars per ton; four foot hard wood, delivered to house, five dollars per cord. All houses are kept in repair by the company.

HOUSES RENTED TO EMPLOYEES BY AHMEEK MINE

HOUSES RENTED TO EMPLOYEES BY ALLOUEZ MINE

This company has 66 frame houses which it rents at the following rates:

4 - 4 room frame dwelling houses at $4.00 per month
8 - 4 room frame dwelling houses at $5.00 per month
2 - 5 room frame dwelling houses at $4.00 per month
18 – 5 room frame dwelling houses at $5.00 per month
2 – 5 room frame dwelling houses at $6.00 per month
2 - 6 room frame dwelling houses at $5.00 per month
2 - 6 room frame dwelling houses at $6.00 per month
2 - 7 room frame dwelling houses at $7.00 per month
26 – 7 room frame dwelling houses at $7.50 per month

The rent includes weekly removal of garbage and the repair of the house. Water is supplied from wells and the company has supplied its employees with soft coal, when requested, at $5.25 per ton, delivered.

The Allouez Mining Company owns 17 log houses for which charges are made as follows:

4 - 5 room log houses at $2.00 per month
10 - 5 room log houses at $2.50 per month
3 - 6 room log houses at $4.00 per month

The Osceola Mining Company owns 79 log houses for which it charges rent as follows:

1 - 4 room log houses at $3.00 per month
61 - 5 room log houses at $3-4.00 per month
12 - 6 room log houses at $4.00 per month
3 – 8 room log houses at $5.00 per month
2 - 10 room log houses at $6.00 per month

HOUSES RENTED TO EMPLOYEES
BY THE OSCEOLA MINE

HOUSES RENTED TO EMPLOYEES
BY THE OSCEOLA MINE

This company owns 267 frame houses which it rents as follows:

```
 3 - 3 room frame dwelling houses at $3.00 per month
29 - 4 room frame dwelling houses at $4.00 per month
129 - 5 room frame dwelling houses at $4-5.00 / month
65 – 6 room frame dwelling houses at $5.00 per month
41 – 7 room frame dwelling houses at $6.00 per month
```

Sixty-five of the above houses are supplied with Lake Superior water from the Calumet Water system, for which a charge of fifty cents per month is made. The other houses are supplied from wells. The rent includes removal of garbage, whenever necessary, and repair of the house. The company sells to its employees, when requested, scrap wood at two dollars per wagonload, delivered, and steam coal at five dollars per ton, delivered. Wherever electric light is used the charge is ten cents per kilowatt per hour.

HOUSES RENTED TO EMPLOYEES
BY THE OSCEOLA MINE

The Wolverine Copper Mining Company. This company has one log house of three rooms which it rents for $3.00 per month. This company has 65 frame houses, from 3 rooms up to 7 rooms in each house, which it rents from $3.50 per month for the 3-room house up to $7.00 per month for the 7-room house, or an average of one dollar per room per month. Water is supplied from wells, and the rent includes the removal of garbage and the general repair of the house. This company supplies its employees, when requested, with fuel at the following rates: hard wood at six dollars per cord, soft coal at five dollars per ton.

The Centennial Copper Mining Company owns 4 4-room log houses which it rents at $2.50 per month and one 5-room log house which it rents at $5.00 per month. It owns 44 frame houses which it rents to employees at an average of one dollar per room per month. Water is supplied form wells and the company has supplied employees, when requested, with soft coal at five dollars per ton.

The Calumet and Hecla Mining Company owns 40 log houses of 4 and 5 rooms each, which it rents at from 50 cents to $3.00 per month. The company owns 764 frame houses for which it charges an average rent of $6.74 per month. None of the houses have fewer than four rooms; 425 of the houses have stone foundations and cement floors in the basements. Lake Superior water is piped to each house by the Calumet & Hecla water system, for which there is no charge, and the rent includes the removal of garbage and the entire repair of the house. This company sells no fuel to its employees except in charity cases, when it is free. The employees who own their own houses, located on lots rented from the company, pay $5.00 per year rental for the lot, which includes water, taxes, and garbage removal.

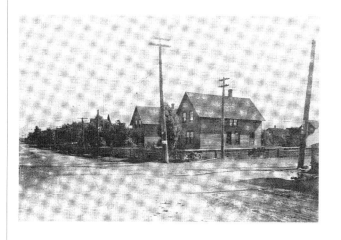

HOUSES RENTED TO EMPLOYEES BY THE CALUMET & HECLA MINE

The Tamarack Mining Company. This company owns 78 log houses and 327 frame houses for which it charges a rental of one dollar per room per month. Most of its houses are supplied with Lake Superior water for which a charge is made of fifty cents per family per month. Rental includes removal of garbage, and whenever electric light is furnished, a charge of six cents per kilowatt hour is made. This company does not supply its employees with fuel.

LaSalle Copper Company owns 4 log houses for which it charges $3.00 per month for a 5-room house, and 6 frame houses for which it charges as follows:

  1 - 8 room frame dwelling houses at $5.00 per month
  2 - 4 room frame dwelling houses at $3.00 per month
  3 - 6 room frame dwelling houses at $6.00 per month

Water is supplied from wells and the company keeps the houses in repair. The company has furnished to employees, when requested, coal at five dollars per ton, delivered.

The Laurium Mining Company. This company owns no dwelling houses.

The Franklin Mining Company. This company owns 13 log houses for which no rent is charged. It owns frame houses for which it charges as follows:

   2 - 3 room frame dwelling houses at $3.00 per month
  12 - 4 room frame dwelling houses at $3.00 per month
  13 - 5 room frame dwelling houses at $4.00 per month
   2 - 6 room frame dwelling houses at $4.00 per month
  19 - 6 room frame dwelling houses at $5.00 per month
   2 - 8 room frame dwelling houses at $5.00 per month

Rent includes removal of garbage and the general repair of the house. This company has supplied its workmen, whenever requested, with soft coal at $4.50 per ton.

The Oneco Copper Mining Company. This company has 8 frame houses which it rents as follows:

1 - 8 room frame dwelling houses at $5.00 per month
7 - 5 room frame dwelling houses at $4.00 per month

Water is supplied from wells and rent includes the removal of garbage, when requested. Fuel is supplied to employees at cost to the company.

The Quincy Mining Company. This company owns 25 log houses which it rents at $1.00 to $2.00 per month. It owns 443 frame houses with 4 to 10 rooms. The average rent of all houses is 80¢ per room per month.

The Hancock Consolidated Mining Company. This company owns no houses. This company is located within the city of Hancock, where most of its employees live. Te city has an adequate water system and the company has supplied to its employees, when requested, fuel at cost to the company.

The Isle Royale Copper Company. This company owns 11 4-room log houses which it rents at $3.00 per month. It owns 109 frame house which it rents at an average of one dollar per room per month. Water is supplied from wells and the rent includes removal of garbage and the general repair of the house. The company has supplied soft coal to its employees, when requested, at five dollars per ton, delivered.

The Superior Copper Company. This company owns no log houses. It owns 16 frame houses which it rents as follows:

2 - 5 room frame dwelling houses at $6.00 per month
2 - 6 room frame dwelling houses at $5.00 per month
12 - 7 room frame dwelling houses at $6.00 per month

All repairs are made at the expense of the company and the water supply is from wells. The company has supplied soft coal to its employees, when requested, at $4.50 per ton, delivered.

The Copper Range Consolidated Company. This company owns no log houses. It owns 607 frame houses, which it rents as follows:

4 - 2 room frame dwelling houses at $1.50 - 2.00 per month
14 - 3 room frame dwelling houses at $2.00 per month
101 - 4 room frame dwelling houses at $2.25 - 4.00 per month
182 - 5 room frame dwelling houses at $3.50 per month
112 - 6 room frame dwelling houses at $5.00 - 7.00 per month
93 - 7 room frame dwelling houses at $4.00 – 6.00 per month
89 - 8 room frame dwelling houses at $4.00 – 12.00 per month
1 - 9 room frame dwelling houses at $12.00 per month
5 - 10 room frame dwelling houses at $6.00 - 10.00 per month
1 - 11 room frame dwelling houses at $6.00 per month
5 - 12 room frame dwelling houses at $15.00 per month

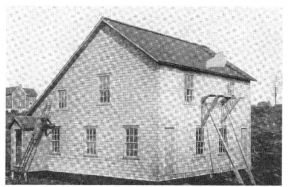

HOUSES RENTED TO EMPLOYEES BY COPPER RANGE CONSOLIDATED MINE

All houses are supplied with water faucets, for which no charge is made. Rent also includes the removal of garbage and the general repair of the house. Where electric light is used a charge of twelve cents per kilowatt hour is made. This company has supplied to its employees, when requested, wood at four dollars per cord and soft coal at $4.50 per ton.

The Winona Copper Company. This company has five log houses of three rooms each, which it rents at $2.00 per month. It owns 115 frame houses, which it rents as follows:

```
38 - 3 room frame dwelling houses at $3.30 per month
 9 - 4 room frame dwelling houses at $3.90 per month
11 - 5 room frame dwelling houses at $4.00 per month
45 - 6 room frame dwelling houses at $5.95 per month
 9 - 7 room frame dwelling houses at $7.45 per month
 3 - 8 room frame dwelling houses at $15.00 per month
```

Water is piped to most of the houses, for which a charge of fifty cents per month is made. Electricity is supplied on a sliding scale of ten cents to seven cents per kilowatt hour. Rent includes removal of garbage, whenever necessary, and the general repair of the house. This company has supplied to its employees, when requested, four foot hardwood at $4.50 per cord.

Company Boarding Houses. None of the companies operates boarding houses.

Company Stores. With the exception of one of the smaller companies, none of the companies operate stores.

The Question of Evictions. During the first month or six weeks of the strike no attempt was made by any of the companies to evict any of the tenants residing on company houses. The first move in this direction was made by one of the companies when it became apparent that the strike was going to last for a considerable time and when the houses were necessary for the men who were working or desired to go to work. At some of the locations men came to the companies who said they were willing to go to work if they could be located within the company lines where they would not be subject to interference or danger, and in order to provide places for such men, some of the striking occupants of company houses were notified that they would have to vacate. At the date of this report [October, 1913] no attempt has been made to evict with the exception of three or four companies who have taken this step for the reasons above stated. At the present time no workman has actually been evicted.

COMPANY HOUSES – SOUTH KEARSARGE

**COMPANY HOUSES
KEARSARGE MINE**

Comparative Tables of Rents Charged in the Michigan and Butte. Montana Mining Districts

TYPE OF HOME	BUTTE MINING AREA	IN THE CITY	COPPER COUNTRY
4 ROOMS	$15-20/MONTH	$17-24/MO.	$3-5/MONTH
6 ROOMS	$28/MONTH	$30-UP/MO.	$5-7.50/MO.

There have been many fine studies made of, and books written about, the 1913 strike. I will not try to settle the issue here. It is obvious, however, that whatever the issues, housing could not have been one of them. In the realm of housing the companies did a masterful job of making it possible for the miners and their families to live in relative safety and comfort – and economy – before the strike.

--- R. Buchko

WHAT OTHER WRITERS AND RESEARCHERS SAY ABOUT COMPANY HOUSING IN THE COPPER COUNTRY:

In his popular *Rebels On The Range*, Arthur Thurner agrees in general with the state of mine housing. He quotes a U.S. labor Department observer that the houses were well-built and kept in good shape. In *Strangers and Sojourners* he referred to the situation as "extremely cheap rents for housing."

On the subject of evictions, Thurner in *Rebels On The Range* states that in November and December some mining companies did start eviction processes. Some workers left voluntarily (many were leaving the Copper Country anyway, since there was no work), and over 600 evictions were stayed by a judge. Calumet & Hecla didn't didn't try to evict strikers or cut off medical benefits until January, 1914 – nearly six months after the strike started. In all, only about a half dozen families were evicted out of the thousands of houses.

Thurner states claims by single men that the housing was unfairly designed for married men with families. This may be true. The company may have felt that married men and men with families would be more stable employees over the long term, because of their responsibilities. Also, since there wasn't enough housing for everyone, men without families were perhaps considered in a better position to fend for themselves than would be those with the burden and expenses of a wife and children.

Thurner suggests that the Copper Country Commercial Club was partial to the companies over the striking miners. This may be somewhat true; in reading their entire publication there's evidence to support that claim. However, research doesn't dispute the facts of the housing situation as reported by this group.

Larry Lankton, in *Cradle To Grave*, looks more skeptically at the housing situation, stating that the companies used it as a form of discrimination. He said, 'The housing situation proved that paternal companies treated some employees like favorite sons and others like bastards" (p.149). The evidence he uses for this is that while the companies provided some 5,000 houses for employees throughout the Copper Country, that did not accommodate all 14,000 workers, which led to some being given housing and others not. That is a fact – one cannot dispute it, and there were many applications for housing whenever a vacancy came up. That these houses were typically given to the employees the company valued the most, leaving out the lowest-paying and most easily replaced of the workers, is unfortunate, but a logical decision on the part of the company. While it would be great if all miners had housing provided at the rates charged, the companies already had spent hundreds of thousands of dollars to build the houses (Calumet and Hecla alone spent over $1 million to build the houses used by employees) and the maintenance and other services provided cost the companies far more each year than was collected in rents. Supplying houses to all miners was, unfortunately, unrealistic; to assign them randomly would be illogical. If it was discriminatory, it was necessarily so.

Lankon agreed that company housing was popular and considered a great benefit. He said, "Housing costs at the Lake Superior copper mines were perhaps the lowest to be found in any major metal-mining district in the country" (p.157).

This article is not an attempt to either validate or refute the conditions surrounding the 1913 strike. The authors mentioned above have done the research and they have written some of the definitive books on the subject. The strike was a complex sequence of events that even these books cannot fully cover. I felt that the subject of housing, however, deserved another look. Whatever the conditions the miners faced, overall those who lived in company houses were satisfied with their living situation, and it was not one of their grievances.

For some of the best work done on copper mining in the Keweenaw, these are four books you'll want to read:

By Arthur W. Thurner:

Rebels On The Range: The Michigan Copper Miners' Strike of 1913-1914. 1984.

Strangers and Sojourners: A History of Michigan's Keweenaw Peninsula. Wayne State University Press, 1994

By Larry Lankton:

Cradle To Grave: Life, Work and Death at the Lake Superior Copper Mines. Oxford University Press, 1991.

Hollowed Ground: Copper Mining and Community Building on Lake Superior, 1840's-1990's. Wayne State University Press, 2010.

CALUMET & HELCA LIBRARY – 1913

OLD KEWEENAW

BY JOSEPH A. TEN BROECK
(From Michigan Pioneer Historical Collections,
Volume 30 – 1904)

Joseph Anthony Ten Broeck, B. D., the son of William P. Ten Broeck and Mary Elizabeth Yundt, was born at La Crosse, Wisconsin, January 4, 1872. The family was of the original Holland stock which settled in the Hudson Valley of New York. He was educated at the Public schools of La Crosse, the University of Minnesota and Seabury Divinity School, and ordained to the ministry of the Protestant Episcopal Church by Bishop Whipple in 1895. In 1901 he took charge of a large field at Christ Church, Calumet including much of Houghton and Keweenaw counties in Michigan, and has since shown a deep interest in collecting details of the early pioneer life of the Copper Country. In 1905 he was married to Clara Daniell, daughter of the late Captain John Daniell organizer of the Tamarack Mine.

The location of Keweenaw Point on the map of Lake Superior is not one whit more unique than the part which it has played in the history of that Lake. Running some fifty miles out into the Lake, it forms a very prominent topographical feature, one whose bold hills and rocky coasts demand attention from the passer-by. The rock strewn shores, broken by safe harbors, have alternately been the terror and the comfort of the storm-tossed mariner. One can imagine with what varying feelings the bold voyageurs of early time looked eagerly for the long finger beckoning to them as they approach, coasting the shore from East or West. If the Lake were rough and stormy, blessings would fall upon its bold head lines which broke the fury of the storm, and on the safe Portage which gave a temporary relief from the unequal struggle. On the other hand, if the wind and weather were favorable, then in true voyageur style curses would fall upon the fortune which added to the already long journey the many miles around the Point or else compelled the tedious Portage. So in like manner, from earliest times, Keweenaw Point has summoned men from afar to explore the regions of Superior and also has repelled them. In prehistoric times it called them perhaps from far-off Mexico for the sake of its copper, and yet by its severe storms of winter forbade their making any permanent stay.

Early records tell us that the first attempt by the white race to reach Lake Superior was made in 1618 by a French voyageur named Brute, who had heard from the Indians of Eastern Canada of the copper to be found in this district. How successful he was history does not say. He did obtain a specimen which was afterwards shown in France and seen by the historian Sagard. (There is a very strong probability that he bought it in an Indian junk shop by the way like many modern travelers to the copper region who stop off at Houghton.) Other explorers set out with the same object before them. It is said that Joliet had this for his ulterior object. However, the detached masses occasionally found along the southern shores of Keweenaw and vicinity, and the inability to reveal their parent source, gave rise to stories of their having been brought from elsewhere, even that they were floated on icebergs across the Lake from Isle Royale. Spasmodic efforts were made to locate the copper, but they proved unsuccessful. In the meantime two hundred years of the history of Lake Superior were passing since its discovery by the white race. And at the end of those two hundred years the Lake promised to be almost as mysterious a wilderness as at the beginning. The missionary had gone up and down the Lake, curing the souls and bodies of the forest dwellers. But he traveled in the same frail canoe which the Indian had used for centuries. Except at a few scattered points like La Point, the Soo or Baraga he had left no permanent mark. Elsewhere he lived like the Indian, sleeping in his wigwam and living on his food. However, by his kindness he was doing a wonderful work in taming the savage nature, so that when the settlers did come the frightful stories of Indian wars and massacres of the East should not be repeated. The story of what the missionary did has been well told.

For many of them were men of education and refinement whose deeds are preserved in the records of the brotherhoods which sent them out.

But there is another band of whom we know but little, and yet who did even more for this section during those two hundred years than the missionary. I refer to the voyageur and the trader. The Hudson Bay Company had various posts established throughout the Northwest. But it was never the policy of the Hudson Bay Company to write history. The wilder the country the better it served the company's purpose. Nor was it policy to publish to the world their transactions. To keep on the right side of the Indians, and to keep the country as wild as possible, were their sole motives. This purpose was well accomplished by the voyageurs and traders. They were a strong, sturdy set, fearless, tire less, determined, inured to hardship. No wilderness was too wild for them to penetrate if furs were to be found there. They ravaged through trackless wilds from the Lake to the Rocky Mountains, then and for years afterwards a *terra incognita* to other whites. Almost the only record of the deeds of these tradesmen is to be found on the bank books of the Hudson Bay Company. They frequently married among the Indians and gave themselves over to the wild life. They met the missionary and led him on his way. And yet this race of men have disappeared like the foam which followed in the wake of their canoes. With muscle like steel from battling with the waves, with eyes like the eagle from looking for the storm, loyal to friend, fierce and bitter toward foes, resourceful in danger, sluggish and reckless when at ease, they skirted quickly along the shore during calm weather, more quickly they dragged their frail canoes upon the beach or sought the safe harbor when the storm gathered. They battled successfully with many storms, but frequently found the storm more than they could master. They have scarcely left a scar on the wilderness. The grass has overgrown their trail through the forest and the wave washed out the mark of their canoe upon the beach: One thing, however, they have done. They left a full knowledge of the shore line of Superior for the first settlers.

And so for two hundred years the white race has visited the inhospitable shores of Lake Superior utterly unprofited by the untold wealth of copper, iron and lumber which lay concealed. Voyageur, trader, missionary, adventurer, a few scattered mission stations, a few old trading posts are all that stand for the work of six generations. The region was entirely as wild as two hundred years before. How is it then that the life of one man has been more than sufficient to see this vast wilderness tamed and the commerce of Lake Superior spring from that of frail canoes to the greatest of the globe? Untold treasure, untold opportunity on every side of mine and forest and commerce and trade? Where is the key and where

the master hand to unlock all this treasure? The key was Keweenaw Point, the hand that of Douglas Houghton.

Almost in a day the Superior district leaped from savagery to civilization. Modern history dates from February, 1841, when he sent out his report of the copper regions. At once men's eyes were opened to the possibilities of that wonderful region; prospectors and miners turned their steps hither from all directions; a new era had dawned or rather, let us say, had burst like a flash of lightning upon the northern sea. That report rang like a clarion call to battle, summoning the host from every land to the conquest of the "Little Brother of the Sea."

Prospector demanded merchants and mechanics. Commerce must be opened up; lumber must be secured, and from one end to the other the Lake took on new life. And yet read the conservative words of the discoverer of the true vein of the copper :

"While I am fully satisfied that the mineral district of our State will prove a source of eventual and increasing wealth to our people, I cannot fail to have before me the fear that it may prove the ruin of hundreds of adventurers who will visit it with expectations never to be realized. I would simply caution those persons who would engage in this business in the hope of accumulating wealth suddenly and without patient industry and capital, to look closely before the step is taken, which will most certainly end in disappointment and ruin. In three years' time great changes were wrought. The country swarmed with persons taking out claims and opening up mines. Every piece of trap rock, copper or no copper, meant a company and stock sold on the market to the highest bidder. A few specimens, so-called, meant a stream of money which might, for all the investor knew, be poured into a lake or swamp. In some locations a trifle better prospect meant more money sunk in larger exploration and better equipment. These inflated prospects threatened to ruin the whole district and led outsiders to pronounce the mines of Lake Superior a humbug. But gradually the inferior mines were weeded out and the country settled down to a reasonable development.

Some curious stories are told of the early attempts at mining. There is one drift pointed out on the lower point, I am told, where the prospector evidently let himself down over the cliff by ropes. A perpendicular wall two hundred feet high drops away from beneath. The shaft was sunk horizontally into the face of the cliff. It was a very wise, unscientific method, because a blast of powder would throw the rocks out into space and there was no trouble with dumps. But where the prospector hung out while the powder was going off I am not told, nor is there the remotest evidence of copper thereabouts. But it was trap rock. (I do not vouch for this story, nor do I know where this prospect is located, nor will I tell you my authority for fear your confidence, like mine, in a certain respectable fellow citizen, be shaken.)

The study of the history of Keweenaw will show that history can be written without blood. In spite of the vast number who visited this section for copper prehistorically, they left no evidences of having been molested hostilely. The relationship between the early voyageurs and Indians was always cordial and friendly. The Indians record only one battle on Battle Island, near Portage entry. There is but one short chapter to tell of man's inhumanity to man amidst the furies of war. A strong lesson may be learned from the cordial and mutual confidence which existed between the pioneers and the aborigines. I say one can learn a strong lesson here as to how to deal with the weaker races; for what a glorious contrast there is between the relationship with the Indian here and in the East. Scourged with fire and baptized with blood were all those eastern lands. In early New England we trace the history of civilization in the blood of the forest dwellers. The colonists met savagery with savagery, blood with blood, fire with fire, until one shudders with horror at the inhumanity of man to man. Certainly they were an uncivilized race, but their deeds and their character seen through the eyes of their bitterest enemies compel our admiration in the desperate struggle against forces whose triumph meant humiliation and annihilation of their own race at the hands of the usurping strangers. They were lovers of freedom, fond of their native soil, true to their ancestral customs, loyal to racial proclivities, faithful unto death to friends, fierce as wolves toward an enemy. Stricken down none mourn their fall and an enemy's hand writes their history.

But thank God, there is no such history to write of the Indian of Keweenaw. Fort Wilkins, established in 1843, proved useless except as a precaution. On several occasions alarms were spread of an uprising, but they were brought in from outside. At one time it was reported at Eagle River that runners were seen going up and down the Eastern shores evidently summoning the tribes to war. The settlers were not particularly concerned but the authorities of the state sent up a supply of guns for use in an emergency. They were the old fashioned flintlock guns even then a little out of date. However they were not entirely useless for they were bought by John Senter, and when the first military company was organized at Calumet were sent hither. The old flint-locks are today stored at Eagle Harbor and also the bayonets once an indispensable adjunct to the war rifle.

At L'Anse there were two or three causeless alarms. On one occasion word was received that the young Indians had taken to the woods with their war weapons. At once the settlers assembled in one house. The men were organized, guns loaded and windows and doors barricaded. Several Indians joined the whites. After several hours of anxious waiting for the expected attack, about eleven o'clock at night friendly Indians were sent out to scout. Some two hours later the glimmer of guns on the hillside in the moonlight indicated the presence of Indians stealthily approaching the house. The terror increased many fold for the crisis had come, but it did not stay however, for these were the scouts returning, and morning light with its natural return of courage, proved the falsity of the alarm and restored the mutual confidence of red and white. One cannot help but admire the men who restrained the savage and cultivated the childlike simplicity of the wild men. They found the Indian truly loyal to the pale-faced brother. He stood ready to guide his canoe and furnish him with the products of the hunt, meat for his hunger, fur for his market, to run his errands and to carry his messages. Over the dying race as seen in Keweenaw we may quote the mutilated inscription on the slab beneath Brockway Mountain near Copper Harbor.

1 *Beneath this slab a red man's body lies.*
2 *Once to his tribe an honor and a prize.*
3 *But death relentless his ------- days hath numbered o'er.*
4 *His bow-string like his bones will carry death no more.*
5 *O stranger! pass not reckless o'er this lonely sod.*
6 *But hesitate and think here lies the*

image of your God.
7 Through wild and savage---------
8 Yet his heart -------------

Compare this with Captain Church's curse over the body of King Philip: "For as much as he has caused many an Englishman's body to lie unburied and to rot above the ground, not one of his bones shall be buried."

The Indians are said never to have had any settlement north of Portage Lake. The birth of the first white child was a cause for great rejoicing. With a curiosity born of native simplicity, old and young, buck and squaw crowded about the hut to catch a glimpse of the white papoose. Bonfires were lighted, dances inaugurated and presents brought. The child was Mrs. Sally Scott, formerly Miss Brockway, born at L'Anse, now living at Lake Linden.

Yet if anyone thinks that it was an easy task to settle in Keweenaw sixty years ago, they are grossly mistaken. Added to the other difficulties which accompany new settlements there was the ungovernable prey of Lake Superior storms. Men might conquer every thing else in the battle for supremacy in the northern wilderness but nothing could stand the fury of a Superior gale. One wonders that men were not discouraged at the attempt to open regular traffic on the lake so frequent were the losses and so great the risk. Captain Hall says that if he had thought he must stay he would have taken a rope and hanged himself.

The story of the opening of the Lake traffic would make a very interesting volume. The canoes of the voyageurs had explored the coastlines so that it was comparatively well known to the navigators, but human mind could not foretell the treachery of the storms nor human skill as yet cope with their violence. So irregular and uncertain were the early boats that for several years travelers were repeatedly obliged to fall back upon the Indian canoes and mackinaws for longer as well as shorter trips. However the establishment of the copper and all other lake industries depended upon the shipping. The battle must be fought to a finish at any cost. Keweenaw demanded attention.

In the summer of 1843, D. D. Brockway and L. B. Charrier, the one a furrier, the other a carpenter in government employ, arrived at the Soo. Their wives are said to have been the first white women west of the Soo. There were at that time but two vessels on the Lake. The *Algonquin* of thirty tons, and the *Furtrader*, a smaller boat, both of them two-masted schooners. After a delay of six weeks, they set sail for L'Anse, where a landing was made August 12, 1843. It was eleven months before another boat arrived and the first news received from the outside world. Two years later Mr. Brockway removed to Fort Wilkins, where he made a permanent residence. Before his arrival, John Hays had, in the year 1844, opened the first successful mine in the region. He found a black oxide of copper of which a specimen is now in the hands of Mr. John Senter of Houghton. His old shaft, seventy-five feet deep, is yet seen a few rods west of the Fort buildings.

But let us return to the shipping interests which the old settlers watched scarcely less eagerly than their prospects. In the Fall of 1844 occurred a disaster of far-reaching importance. The *Astor* was ten days overdue at the Soo. The *Algonquin* arrived with the sad news that, having anchored in Copper Harbor, she was struck by a terrific gale and wrecked on the rocks near Fort Wilkins. It was a far-reaching catastrophe for the growing settlements along the coast which were waiting for her to bring their winter supplies. They faced great peril and suffering during the bitter season now approaching. The *Algonquin* had all that she could do to supply Fort Wilkins. However, it was once more demonstrated that heroic courage, (if it has sense enough to lie by until a Lake Superior storm blows over) can overcome every obstacle. The canoe and the mackinaw boat did much to alleviate conditions, but another such disaster at that time would have almost emptied the country of inhabitants. The addition of steamers to the lake shipping was another result of the strenuous demands which the opening up of the copper interests was making upon commerce for better and larger boats. Thirty-six years after Robert Fulton launched his first steamer, they were plying the waters of the northern sea. Captain Averill of Chicago, tradition says, conceived the idea of shipping grain direct from Chicago to Europe. He built a boat for the purpose, three hundred and sixty-five tons burden, a propeller called the *Independence*. In those days, like the pudding of the proverb, the test of a boat was in its using. Its sea-worthiness and speed were matters of skill and not of scientific ship-building and consequently unknown until put to the test. The *Independence* reached the remarkable speed of five miles an hour. If loaded to her utmost capacity with coal she would travel one-half way across the Atlantic before the supply ran out. Consequently the captain sent her to the Superior trade under his son, Captain A. J. Averill. She was dragged across the straits and launched, the first steamer to float on the surface of Lake Superior. At the time of her crossing quite a fleet was being dragged over, mostly if not all besides her being sailers. The *Independence* made only one trip that fall of 1845, and this was by no means propitious. It has been minutely described by Lewis Manville, the steward. She landed at Copper Harbor, touched at Eagle Harbor, where there were but few houses. While discharging cargoes at Eagle River dock, a storm threatened which caused the Captain to leave at once for La Pointe without finishing the unloading, expecting to finish on the return trip. After a stormy voyage, the vessel almost reached La Pointe, when suddenly it was struck by a severe storm and driven back until by good fortune a safe refuge was found under the lee of Keweenaw Point. It returned to Eagle River and then on to La Pointe. Later new engines were put into the boat which increased its speed sixty per cent, or to eight miles an hour. After battling successfully with many a fierce storm and outriding many a violent blast, she came to an inglorious end by exploding at the Soo. In spite of Mr. Manville's statement to the contrary, it seems that the *Julia Palmer* was the second steamer on the Lake, but according to records at Eagle river and the memory of John Senter, Mr. Manville would put the *Napoleon*, launched in the fall of 1845, ahead of the Julia Palmer. It is true that the Napoleon was portaged across the Soo that fall, but as a sailer, knocked down. A few years later she was equipped as a steamer. The *Julia Palmer* was a sidewheeler, one hundred feet long, thick set, could drift to perfection before the severest gale with plenty of sea room but utterly unable to make head against a gale, or even to control her own movements. On August 28, 1846, she landed for the first time at Eagle River, having on board Mrs. M. E. W. Sherwood of New York, the authoress, and Mr. John Senter, whose personality plays such a large part in the history of Keweenaw.

On her last trip the staunch boat met and successfully outrode one of those furious hurricanes which make men feel their impotency in the presence of the forces of nature. In the fall of 1847 she set sail for the Soo with winter supplies for the Point. When but a short way out, a fearful storm came on from the East. An effort was made to get behind White Fish Point, but it failed. On the wind hurled the helpless boat beyond the shelter of Presque Isle. It was no human hand that saved her from being dashed to pieces on the rocks near the present Marquette. The smoke stack was down, a monkey-wrench held the machinery together, everything was cast overboard that could be dispensed with; pork and lard, so essential to the comfort of the settlers, were thrown into the furnaces to help in the present crisis; the stove was bottom side up where it formerly stood. With each plunge everything moveable was hurled violently about and huge mountains of water swept the decks from end to end with relentless fury. The captain and the mate, Jack Angus, held a council as the locality of the vessel. The mate declared in Keweenaw Bay, the captain off Copper Harbor. Which was right will never be known, for the next land sighted was Isle Royale. An effort to enter Rock Harbor proved unsuccessful, but finally, the storm abating, a landing was made at Slate Island. Here the wood supply was replenished with the aid of hand and wood saws; for all the axes were at the bottom of the Lake. Copper Harbor was reached sixteen days out from the Soo. And when one adds to the story of this appalling struggle, the scarcity of food which resulted during that winter for the settlers owing to the loss of provisions, one wonders at the courage which still persisted in the fight till the campaign should be won.

If time permitted, one might give many more illustrations of what the opening of this country involved. I have barely touched on the subject, but certainly it is a story worth rehearsing accurately and to its fullest extent. The courage and skill in such a frontier life is well worthy of emulation and would serve as a stimulant to our lives of ease, and the actors deserve remembrance at our hands. The eastern states today at great cost are trying to make up neglected records of their foundings. We should profit by their mistakes. Complete files of old newspapers, hand-bills, private letters of public interest, store-accounts, hotel registers and others records of current events should be put on file beyond danger from fire and under State protection. I am told that there is but one lone specimen of Keweenaw copper at Lansing in the State Museum. Memories of old settlers should be pumped dry, not more for facts than for conditions of early time. The time to act is now. Something has been done, much is left undone. Keweenaw occupies too important a place in the history as well as on the map of Lake Superior to be passed by unnoticed, or to allow those men who mastered its wilderness to take an obscure place in the history of the north. They unlocked the treasures of the richest regions on the globe; they forced the opening of the greatest commerce on the globe. Certainly the study of their lives, their methods, their characters and their mistakes would be a source of great profit.

There is one more motive to lead to an attempt to preserve more accurately the history of Keweenaw Point. History, especially early history, has always proven of great value to the man of letters. One needs but to run over a list of our own great literary work to discover how many of them were inspired by the tale of by gone years. The simplicity and open-heartedness of pioneer life strongly appeals to the mind of the author. Need I mention Homer's Iliad, the greatest of poems, resting on the legends of early Greece, or the Eneid of Virgil, or the Cid, or the poems of the later poets of England inspired by the simplicity of rural life, probably what is more to the point, the works of Washington Irving. How many of his quaint stories are built upon the tales which he has gathered from the hills and dales of the Hudson Valley, and by a master hand has polished into gems of literature, only those can know who have delved into his old haunts. Tales whose value, like a diamond in the rough, his quick eyes recognized and his skilled hands have polished. We owe many of Washington Irving's choicest stories not only to his masterful pen but also to those who have preserved the anecdotes.

Has not Keweenaw a stock of tales waiting to be worked over by one who has the genius? Slip up along side of some old settler and gain his confidence. Bead in the empty stare of vacant houses the story of shattered hopes and broken prospects, of life, of death, of love, of courtship, of friendship, of marriage, of happy homes and sacred memories. Go among the tombs, the silent resting places of the dead; read there, the story of agony and mourning. Read the trite sayings promising undying remembrances. But time, the ruthless destroyer, has already nearly erased the legend and crumbled the monument. Even the tombstones have their witty side. Who has not heard the sad story, with its many variations, of Johnny drowned in or off Copper Harbor, which, will take a higher critic of the German school to unravel? Was he sailor or miner, drunk or sober, does his body lie beneath the icy waters or are his mortal remains laid at peace beneath the warm sod at the foot of Brockway Mountain and where his wooden monument now stands, sharing his grave as well as his slab with the aforesaid Indians?

"Friends may weep o'er where I sleep
Or where my name is found,
And brother dear may drop a tear
For Johnny who was drowned."

Such is the sentiment, composed by his brother, inscribed with black paint on pine wood by McLain, a carpenter. For I think you will find on investigation that when it comes to story telling for the sake of amusement, the story tellers of Keweenaw Point have learned well that time-honored motto of all good story tellers; "Never spoil a good story for the sake of the truth."

REMINISCENCES OF "OLD KEWEENAW"
BY MRS. W. A. CHILDS, CALUMET.

(From Michigan Pioneer Historical Collections, Volume 30 – 1904)

In the year 1836 Michigan claimed jurisdiction over a strip of land also claimed by Ohio, but Congress agreed to admit Michigan to the Union upon condition that she relinquish her claim to the disputed territory and accept a larger tract of country in the Upper Peninsula. Included in this area was the land lying north of Torch Lake, known as Keweenaw Point, Isle Royale and several smaller islands. The word Keweenaw being derived from the Indian word "Ki-wi-wee-noning," meaning the place where the portage ends, or the canoe is carried back to the lake. Burdened thus by what was considered worthless territory, Michigan, on January 26, 1837, became the thirteenth State of the Union. Shall anyone say that thirteen is an unlucky number? Seven years later the government sent a farmer, a carpenter, and a blacksmith to the Indian reservation on Keweenaw Bay. Their mission was not simply to teach the Indians how to work, but also to instruct them how to live as white people live.

Dr. Douglas Houghton, state geologist of Michigan, made the first scientific examination of the country in 1841. His explorations and his life were suddenly ended by the swamping of his canoe in the lake near Eagle River.

October 13, 1845, the first protestant missionary was settled at Kewawenon mission, about three miles up the shore from L'Anse. At this time the Rev. W. H. Brockway was superintendent of the Indian mission of Lake Superior. He it was who sent the Rev. Pitezel to take charge of the mission at L'Anse in 1844. This reverend gentleman was a personal friend of my father's family, and always made our home his headquarters when making visits as presiding elder to different towns at least ten years later. I, as a small child, have heard him many times tell of his experiences on land and water.

The life of a pioneer in a wild country is far from being monotonous. He is continually coming in contact with extremes. His life is not all made up of thorns, nor of clouds and storms. Often it is the case that in new and unsettled portions of the country the travels and labors of the missionary form an important link in its after history, and unless the missionary makes the record it is not likely to be made by others. Much of the history of our State has been gleaned from the writings of Mr. Pitezel.

The Cliff Mine was the first to begin operations. Three years were spent in developing it with discouraging results. At the end of that time the mine changed hands, and under control of new owners proved to be very rich in copper and silver, and eventually paid $7,000,000 in dividends. To make money was the object which induced most of the pioneers to forego the blessings of home in a better land, and endure the privations of the wilderness. Many of the miners had families in distant lands, some across the seas, whose society they had not enjoyed for years. The influences which surrounded them tended to harden them. Many abandoned themselves to drinking and gambling; vice and wickedness prevailed, yet under the rough exterior were some noble minds and generous hearts. These people of the long ago in their attire were odd specimens of humanity; flannel shirts, mackinaw coats, and shoepacks were full-dress for a long time. Frequently a man had no coat at all, and if cold added a few more shirts. I recall the costume of one man who was commonly called the *dude* of the place. His favorite shirt was blue flannel, heavily embroidered in silks of different colors on bosom and collar, his trousers white duck, for comfort worn over heavy ones of flannel, held at the waist by a red sash, on his feet he wore top-boots; on his head a stovepipe hat. I assure you, he dresses quite differently now as one of the wealthy men of the iron country.

We received mail in those days sometimes twice in a winter, brought overland from Green Bay on dogtrain, which would also carry the provisions and blankets of the carrier, he walking on snow shoes. The train or sled was constructed very much like the toboggan of the present day, the provisions, blankets and mailbags being lashed fast to the bottom with strong cord. Sometimes three dogs would perform the service of hauling this mail-train.

In 1844 adventurers began to pour into the country from eastern states. Mining operations commenced at various places along the shore on Keweenaw Point. Copper Harbor was the central point of excitement for all. The shore was lined with the tents of prospectors and miners, and Mr. D. D. Brockway, whom we have before mentioned as the blacksmith sent by the government to Kewawenon, hoping to better his fortunes, removed with his family to Copper Harbor, his only means of transportation being an open boat. The wind blew a gale, the lake was all agitation, and our friends were forced to land and dry themselves and their goods by a log fire before they could sleep. This same year Mr. Brockway and his Indian voyagers barely escaped death when bringing a boat load of potatoes from L'Anse. At a later time he had a long boat and a smaller one filled with hay he had cut at Agate Harbor; a bridge uniting the boats was also piled high with hay; a sudden squall drove them helpless to the rocky shore, but providentially the great waves lifted them on to a large flat rock and receding left them there; they were now in danger of losing the boats, but succeeded in making them fast to a tall tree, after which they walked home to the joy of the family who had counted them lost.

Fort Wilkins, named for Major Wilkins who figured conspicuously in the war with the Indians at the siege of Detroit, was built in 1844-45. Two Companies of soldiers arrived in 1845 on an old propeller which had been brought over the portage at the Sault the year previous. The soldiers remained two years, and were then sent to participate in the war with Mexico. In the rear of the Fort, a hundred or two yards distant, in a gloomy wood of birch and fir, is the burying place of the Fort. The marks of many graves can be seen among the trees, which of course have sprung up since. Some graves have been opened and the bones removed to more desirable quarters, but they have no historical association connected with them.

Copper Harbor was a government reservation, but when it became apparent there was no need of a fort, most of the land was put upon the market. Mr. Brockway got his by pre emption claim, and on this land stood the town of Copper Harbor. Not far from the Harbor is Brockway mountain standing guard over the dark waters below, with a few stunted trees thinly clothing its nakedness. Behind it stretches away a long train of inferior hills, all of which have in their day witnessed the passage of noble ships, and there is not an echo on either that has not answered to the crack of rifle or scream of whistle. It was very hard to get material and supplies for want of transportation, though there were several vessels, and in this year a second steamer was put into service, the *Julia Palmer*; this steamer one year later encountered a terrific storm, being blown all over Lake Superior, but finally, after three weeks, came into port to the surprise of everyone. Many of the pioneers of the whole country were on board; one gentleman found steps being taken to administer his estate. The first steamer on the great lake was the *Independence*, and we are told it was built for trading with England, but as she could make but four miles an hour, and a whole cargo of coal would take her only half way across the Atlantic, she was strengthened and improved to run six miles an hour, and put into Lake Superior. One lady says she still remembers the little tub with her one mast, her piratical blackness, and, oh! Her awful rolling.

Supplies of every kind were procured in the fall to last till navigation should open. Sometimes the last boats would be wrecked, or sometimes encounter storms, making it necessary to throw provisions overboard, pork and ham even being used for fuel to make steam to propel the boat. There was necessarily considerable suffering before winter passed and the white sail was again seen in the distance, which brought a fresh supply from below. One year the potatoes had been consumed, flour nearly gone, fish could not be gotten because of the great thickness of the ice, game taken from the woods was inadequate, and many of the miners were almost reduced to starvation. One man more resourceful than some made a small mill in which he ground the corn that should have been fed to the chickens. This meal was made into mush three times a day and given to the children to eat with molasses. When the Sault Canal was opened in 1855 it put Copper Harbor on what was the highway between New York and Minnesota. These were days of long distances, slow going freight and no refrigeration. There was little butter and less milk, but what matter when the palate was not accustomed to taste of these.

As the number of the boats increased so did the comforts of the people. Fresh meats and apples were among the luxuries that found their way into the home of the pioneer. In autumn, when cold enough to carry meat without too great danger of spoiling, it was an amusing sight to see steamers come into port with the carcasses of sheep and sides of beef hanging from upper and lower decks. These were sold in halves or quarters, cut into suitable shape for cooking and carefully packed in snow to be used as occasion demanded.

Apples were so rare that they could

only be indulged in by the few who were considered affluent. I recall that one particular barrel found its way into a house at Copper Harbor. One evening quite a number of friends had gathered for social intercourse, and as a treat a large plate of apples was brought out. One little girl sat quietly by and saw the apples passed to one and another of the older people, and thinking how lovely when one of these bright red apples would be given her. Finally the looked for moment arrived and she was invited to take one. With eyes glowing bright and cheeks rosy she took one. She was then asked to take another, which she innocently did. Then asked to take another, and another till her little lap was full, her eyes dancing with pleasure, and cheeks outshining those of the apples. Finally she heard a snicker go around the room and realized she had been made the butt of the company. Burning with shame she settled back into the corner of the old lounge on which she sat, and the apples one by one rolled to the floor. It is needless, to say she ate no apples that night, nor could she be persuaded to touch another that whole long winter.

Woman has been found to bear her share of the toil, privations and dangers connected with the struggles of the pioneer. She finds herself environed by sights and sounds to her entirely new, and strange. She may be surrounded by few of her own language and manner of life; perhaps she is alone, except the members of her own family. At first it seems most romantic, and there is a peculiar charm about it all, but the spell is at last broken and the scene begins to wear an aspect of monotony. Her body is in the forest, but her mind is with loved ones far away. Her domestic cares are onerous and trying, and if everything else differs about her, she must have her home regulated as much as possible after the old sort. She is expected to be nurse, cook, housekeeper, seamstress and governess, while a man thinks he does well if he is a specialist in one line. After everything is in order she takes up knitting or sewing as a respite from more active toil. Now Indians come to the door, and without knocking, open it and walk in. The men usually seat themselves on chairs or benches, while the squaws, with their papooses, sit on the floor. The men are sure to be smoking tobacco or *kinnikinic*, and for a time it is puff and spit. All this time the odor from the dirty blankets and steaming moccasins is nearly smothering the lady of the house. After a while the head man of the tribe, more important than the others, begins to talk in Indian and succeeds in making her understand that they came for pork or bread, and that they must have it, too. In sympathy with the hungry, and sometimes fearing for her life she gives them what may be left from the last baking, and they are sent away only to return in a few weeks for more. At certain seasons of the year they have been known to bring offerings of game or fish, and by unmistakable signs let it be known that anything would be acceptable in return.

Once an Indian brought to a certain housewife a mocock of maple sugar, containing perhaps ten pounds, which he wished to exchange for flour. This she was willing to do; then came the question of what to put it in for transportation. She had nothing that could be spared. He evidently had, for off came his shirt, into it went the flour, and away went the Indian with a happy farewell. On another occasion, having grown tired of salt pork, the only meat she had eaten for months, she asked the Indians if they could not bring her something from the forest. They expressed themselves willing to try, and in a few days returned bringing a beaver's tail.

The first lighthouse was built at Copper Harbor, about 100 feet from where the one on Hayes Point now stands. It was built of rock in the form of a circular tower, 70 feet high. The second on Manito, a facsimilie of the first. By the erection of these lights a great benefit was conferred on mariners and the traveling public generally. Prior to the erection of these lights the only beacon was a globe lamp sent out in a yawl boat and placed upon a lone rock in the channel, to give notice of impending danger. One man by the name of Smith was among the first to take charge of the light on Manito. It is said that he one day in June, 1856, rowed out to welcome the first boat of spring, after a long and dreary winter on the island, and to learn something of the outside world. Among other things he was told that Buchanan had been elected to the presidency the previous November.

Have you ever thought, in your protected modern home, what it must have been to have lived far away from the heart of things? How one's ideas of even the necessities change under stress!

We do not like to look back on the past as a better period than the present, but certainly there were no strikes or lockouts, no new women or social problems, no women's clubs.

THE WALL OF SILVER MINE: UNDISCOVERED TREASURE OR "UNCLE NED" STORY?

UNCLE NED STORY: An historian's term for a terrific tale, but one which lacks documentation, based on something someone heard from someone else; such as, "My Uncle Ned knew Jesse James, and he said...; Uncle Ned was given a ring that he was told belonged to George Washington....My Uncle Ned knew a guy who was there when Lincoln was shot, and he saw a second gunman..." The stories are not always impossible to believe, and some might even be true, but most are false, and almost all will remain unprovable.

The Wall of Silver Mine is a newer legend, but has gained a lot of popularity since the 2004 publication of the book *Wall of Silver* by Richard Kellogg. In fact, that book is the only known source of information about the supposed mine.

The story goes that in the 1700's England sent an expedition to the U.P. to locate silver to restock its depleted treasury. The man charged with the expedition not only found silver (*and* battled Indians *and* saved the chief's daughter *and* married her, etc.), but found the mother lode, including a wall of almost pure silver. After a few years of mining, the expedition met with illness and disaster and the mine was forgotten – until 1927 when a geologist/prospector found it. Finding the Wall of Silver Mine made the man rich, but he never revealed the location of the mine until just before his death, and the person to whom he revealed it didn't mine much silver, didn't cash in the millions of gold he stashed there, didn't sell his knowledge of the mine's location to anyone – he simply wrote a book that is published and sold locally.

By now you see my skepticism. In fact, the story of the *Wall of Silver,* as written, has no credibility. The story is fantastic in the telling, but doesn't stand up to logic or research:

- The adventures of the English geologist are such that would make John Smith and Pocahontas jealous. That's not to say it *cannot* be true, but why can't we find this amazing tale anywhere but in this book?

- Shipments of rich and immensely valuable ore were supposedly sent to England, and yet when the mine met with trouble, it was simply abandoned and forgotten. This mine was no ordinary mine, but had the purest silver ever found in the history of man, plus a crystal wall of gold and gems worth millions – yet it was quickly abandoned and forgotten?

- According to the author, when the mine was rediscovered in 1927 the first shipments were sold (illegally) to the mafia in Chicago, and paid for with $35,000 in gold pieces. Supposedly these gold pieces were left in the mine, never cashed in. Why would such risks be taken, never to benefit?

- Names throughout the book have allegedly been changed, so it is impossible to verify the identities involved in the story – past or present.

- Even if we had the names, for some reason the author waited until all the people had passed away, and were unable to confirm or deny his claims.

- Even the underworld crime family is just called "Chicago family" in the book, for "safety." How does the name of a crime family from over 80 years ago pose a danger?

• The discoverer of the mine in 1927 supposedly became a millionaire (even though he never cashed in his gold or mined much silver); the author he revealed it to received $5,000 in gold pieces and knew where the rest was (by then worth millions), yet not only did he never take out the gold from the mine, according to him he never even opened the sealed bags with the fortune in gold pieces.

• The location of the mine is not revealed, except to say that it is on private property. In other words, not only can no one find it, to try would include trespassing.

• The author offers supporting documents, but the events he supports do nothing for the credibility of the story. He shows a picture of barrels which he says he was told contained silver ore (but which could contain marshmallows); he shows documents which shows he ran for public office in 1970 (so what?); he shows that he tried to obtain other documents, but because he couldn't remember the exact date, those documents weren't available; he shows what the value of gold would be today, but anyone can find that in a hobby magazine. It was as though he needed to offer evidence to substantiate *something,* so he grabbed *anything.* The evidence that would have been helpful – the journals of the geologist from the 1700's, names that could be verified, silver ore from the mine, the roll of counterfeit coins that "Chicago Family" made with his silver, a response from *anyone* – are either lost, unavailable, or not offered.

The idea behind the book is exciting, and although it is not a masterpiece (the dialogue is as unbelievable as the events), it's an engaging story. If it were true, it would be a monumental event. Perhaps it is true --- I would be glad to be completely wrong, for the sake of the area and the sake of history. However, there's nothing to support the story, and there are so many holes in the logic that I believe we have a pure and tangible Uncle Ned right here in the Keweenaw. We have a tale designed to do exactly what it has done: create a group of avid searchers throughout the Keweenaw every summer, looking for the lost mine. P.T. Barnum would be proud.

Mr. Kellogg wrote an interesting story of history, discovery, intrigue, conspiracy, murder, and more ---- but it's a story.

BUT IS IT POSSIBLE?

HISTORY RECORDS A "CEILING OF SILVER"

> My personal skepticism about the *Wall of Silver* story doesn't mean such a thing is impossible. This article from the *Sunday Herald* of Boston, Dec. 4th, 1881, suggests that such a treasure trove is far from impossible. From its discovery in 1868 until 1884 when water filled Silver Islet mines and it was felt the mine's best days were over, more than $3 million in silver was taken from the Earth. In 1919 and again in the 1970's unsuccessful attempts were made at re-opening the Silver Islet Mine.

(From *Michigan Pioneer Historical Collections Vol. 4* - 1883)

SILVER ISLET

HOW A REMARKABLE MINE WAS DISCOVERED – SOME PECULIARITIES OF SUPERIOR SHORES --- A ROOF WORTH HALF A MILLION.

From the Sunday Herald, Boston, Mass., December 4, 1881.

It is not unusual, in these days of speculation and marvelous financial operations, to listen to stories of the wildest recklessness in these directions, confounding to the inexperienced and astounding to the conservative mind. Almost always it is the transactions in stocks or securities connected with mines, railroads, and different forms of corporate interests, rather than the physical appearance of these interests, that attract attention. Thus a copper mine, situated in the midst of a region which abounds in these manifestations, is common-place affair enough, and may present but few features which will render even the most graphic description interesting. But the story of the operations of a giant manipulator, in connection with the securities of this mine, may command the attention of the world.

Occasionally, however, there are peculiarities in the situation, character, or development of these interests which are equal to, or perhaps overshadow, any financial transactions with which they may become associated. Such instances are usually worthy of special scrutiny and investigation, as belonging to the class of things in this world - some knowledge of which is worth having. To this class the writer believes the *Silver Islet* mine to belong, and something of its history and description will be here given, not so much as illustrating the financial operations to which it has given rise, as to call attention to the features of this morsel of natural production, and become better acquainted with one of the wonders of North American possession.

DISCOVERY

The shores of Lake Superior long

ago became a wonder to geologists, and the seekers after mineral wealth have been often confounded no less at the abundance of precious ores secreted there, than by the unexpected conditions under which it has been discovered. Especially is this true of portions of the north, or Canada, shore of this great inland sea, although, as yet, the investigations seem to stand only upon the threshold of the immense storehouse existing.

In July, 1868, a party of mining engineers cruising along the shores of Thunder Bay, when just off the point of Thunder Cape, sailed along by a little islet of rock, close in upon the shore. This island was about three-quarters of a mile from the mainland, and measured about ninety feet each way across, and rose out of the lake only about eight feet in the highest part. It may be noticed that the members of this exploring party were not extremely sanguine [hopeful or confident] as to discovering rich ore deposits in the Thunder Bay region, because they had noted that the rock about was mostly composed of grayish flags and red and white sandstones, lying in a horizontal position, and they had been accustomed to expect valuable finds in highly inclined and crystalline rocks. However, it was also remembered that some unusually fine copper deposits had been found in the horizontal formation of the Superior shores, and they kept their eyes open in consequence, willing to be convicted by the logic of facts of making

a mistaken valuation.

Numbers of the party landed upon this rocky islet, and began picketing for a line of mining operations which had been established on shore. A vein of ore and galena [lead sulfide] was soon noted, and nuggets of metallic silver were found, close to the water's edge. A single blast detached all the vein rock above the surface of the water which carried ore; but farther out, where the rock was submerged, black patches with a greenish tinge could be plainly seen following the vein. In short, this vein was soon proved to abound in silver of extraordinary richness. At once this rock was christened *Silver Islet* - an appellation which it has proved to merit.

SILVER ISLET – ON THE NORTH SHORE OF LAKE SUPERIOR

THE SITUATION

Silver Islet is much exposed to

storms from the west, southwest, and east, and the storms of that region are storms indeed. The course of the vein discovered traversing the island proved to be about north 35° west, and its dip about 85° southeast, its greatest width being on the northwest side of the islet. The metallic minerals of the vein and branches were found to be silver, silver glance, tetrabedrite, donacykite, galena, blende, iron and copper pyrites, cobalt bloom and nickel green. The rock intersected by the silver vein is a chloritic diosite, forming andike, differing somewhat from other dikes of this location, among which are corsyte and anorthite porphyry.

In the year following the discovery of Silver Islet (1869) the summer was very stormy, and not much progress was made in excavating the rock. In August of that year the sinking of a shaft was begun, from which it was intended to cross-cut to the vein as the shaft descended. During this year buildings were erected in the islet and all mining operations were established. The sinking of a shaft was for a time discontinued on account of the influx of water. Blasting under water was successful, and extended over about thirty feet of the vein. In the winter of 1869-70 there was taken from Silver Islet by ten men in fourteen days of actual work, $16,000 worth of ore, a fact which attracted much attention wherever mining operations are noted, as it signified a mine of unusual richness. In September, 1870, operations were begun to establish a permanent mine at Silver Islet. Extensive breakwaters were built, part of the vein inclosed by a coffer dam, the area within the latter pumped dry, considerable mining done, and seventy-seven tons of ore were shipped before the close of navigation, or in about four weeks of running. The winter of 1870-1 was very stormy. In February severe gales were experienced, and the floating ice tore away cribwork for 250 feet in length, chafed the ends of large logs so that they looked like brooms, and iron bolts two inches in diameter were twisted off. The cofferdam was filled up in a very short time after the cribbing was destroyed, but the dam itself sustained little damage. By the 1st of May, 1871, an excavation had been made in the rich part of the vein inclosed by Silver Islet. the coffer-dam, leaving a length of sixty-five, depth of thirty-two, and an average width of eight feet. At the close of navigation in November this depth had increased to ninety feet. The total production of Silver Islet from time of discovery until close of navigation in 1871 was $763,400.59.

VICISSITUDES[1]

In the winter of 1873-4 the terrible storms again made their appearance. On December 1 a southeaster tore away 350 feet in length of submerged cribs, caused a loss of 20,000 feet of timber and seven

---

1 A change of circumstances, usually not positive or well-received.

and one-half tons of bolts, and carried away the upper portion of the main breakwater. The breakwater had an altitude of nearly twenty feet above the level of the lake. Eight feet in height of the top and sixty feet in length of it was carried away. Rocks were hurled around the islet like hailstones, and the buildings were considerably damaged. The ore produced from 1872 to 1875 was of estimated value $1,195,718.45.

From the time of discovery to the present, considerably more than $3,000,000 worth of silver has been taken from Silver Islet, and it has paid to proprietors upward of $1,600,000, beside all the expenses of its development and working. Ten levels now intersect the main shaft of the mine, and these extend for hundreds of feet, even far out under the lake bottom. But the finding of the *bonanzas*, which seem to constitute the principal deposits of this mine, have been at intervals often of considerable time, and there have been singular alternations of tremendous outlay and hope almost given up on the part of the owners, and rich finds which would recompense almost in a single day the outlay and labor of years. Some of the operations necessary in developing this mine have been singular enough.

In excavating the mine below the surface of the island a portion of rock was left intervening between the lake and excavated portion, which formed a barrier or roof, the only means of keeping the water of the lake from flooding the mine. The roof or canopy, as viewed from within the mine, presents the appearance of a vast vaulting or arch of silver, so thickly is it strewn with the pure metal. It is estimated that $500,000 worth of pure silver is thus in sight of the upward looker in the top of the mine, all included in a comprehensive gazing upon the inside of this roof. It was determined at one time to remove this roof, and appropriate the silver to the further development of the mine. To accomplish this without destroying the mine, it was decided to construct an artificial roof, sixty feet below the surface of the lake, to be built of heavy brick arches, spanning the drifts or excavations of the east and west veins throughout their entire length (132 feet at that level) with a brick chimney or shaft enclosing the present shaft, and giving means of communication with the mine below. When these arches and shaft should be completed, and proven by the hydrostatic test of permitting the intervening space to be filled to the lake surface, it was intended to withdraw that water, and *stope* or excavate from underneath, thus securing the rich material of the roof.

COUNTER DEVELOPMENTS

But this proceeding became for a time unnecessary, in consequence of the discovery of another bonanza no less than $700,000 worth of almost pure silver being taken out of one pocket. Thus it has been with this mine. Bonanzas and pockets are discovered at intervals, rivaling in richness any known silver mines in the world, while the great expense of working the mine and the peculiarities of the situation render the history of the enterprise a curious alternation between long continued and exhaustive labor and outlay, and unbounded success. And these conditions promise to return with more marked emphasis in future. Meanwhile, parties directly interested in Silver Islet have most unbounded faith in its excelling any other silver mines known in the future, while the uncertainties connected with the matter, and the element of probable success connected with the certainty of great outlay, renders the enterprise a favorite investment even with capitalists not inclined to be fanciful or misled in financial matters.

Another physical peculiarity of Silver Islet is worth recording. On December 28, 1875, while a party of men were engaged in drilling a hole in the end of the drift on the eighth level the drill broke through a crevice, or "vug." Water at once flowed through the aperture, and one of the miners took a candle to look into the drill hole, not being aware that there was a large escape of gas with the water. The gas instantly took fire, sending out a flame into the drift for more than forty feet. The men threw themselves along the bottom of the drift, and remained uninjured, and the flame soon subsided when they escaped by the shaft. Returning again into the drift, when within forty feet of the end, the gas again ignited, filling the drift with flame to within three feet of the bottom, the flame extending along the back of the drift 150 feet towards the shaft. Some time after the men walked through the drift without a light, and filled the drillhole with a wooden plug. On the following day no gas was discovered in the drift until a candle was brought close to the plug, when the gas again took fire, giving a jet about a foot long, which has been burning ever since. This probably indicates, say the geologists, that the rocks near Silver Islet are of much more recent age than has been generally supposed.

So, with a ceiling of silver recorded by history, is a wall of silver impossible? Absolutely not. It's likely that many walls of silver exist in the Lake Superior region. It's the particular story of the book *Wall Of Silver* that doesn't hold water. It is possible that the author of the book used this historical information as the basis for an interesting fantasy – in the absence of real evidence, that's my conclusion.

THANK YOU, BUT NO COMEBACK NEEDED

I find myself laughing, in a "Geez, not again!" way, when I hear and read about how America is "coming back," about how we're "down but not out." and looking for a "rebirth." A few of the recent Super Bowl ads implied that we're at halftime and behind in the game.

Not even close. We're still winning.

I ask myself if people even pay any attention to what is going on around them, if they can believe we're losing some battle for supremacy. There's no need for a rebirth, a comeback, or a new direction. Sure, we

have economic work to do, political work to do, a lot of environmental work to do, and many issues and challenges ahead – but without exception there's no better place to be than the United States Of America. It's not perfect – but *news flash* – it never has been! The so-called innocent age of the 1950's and early 1960's was full of Cold War fears, cancer epidemics, the beginnings of Vietnam, and yes, even unemployment problems. The age of peace and love was full of racism, violence, war, and yes – economic issues. You cannot find an age where there weren't as many problems as there were things to celebrate, and today is no different. At the end of the day, however, you're living in a place where a teenager doesn't face three years in jail because he kissed a girl (which is happening right now in the U.A.E.); you don't live in a place where the government massacres thousands of its own people because they are ethnically different; you can say what's on your mind, and that right is guaranteed. A woman who bares her arms is not put in prison, or worse. You can show your children the uniform of a police officer and say, "If you need help, he/she will be there for you. He/she cares." You can look at your armed forces and know that the vast majority serve honorably and faithfully – and those who don't are not tolerated. You can have an openly gay son or daughter (as I do) and not worry that she will be arrested for her lifestyle. You are not limited by caste, by color, by religious beliefs, or by your background.

I am reminded of a story I was told

on the eve of the 2008 election. The person who relayed it, an American military officer overseas, was discussing the close presidential campaign, and noted out loud that whichever candidate won, about half the country would be unhappy about it. The person with whom he was talking in that Mediterranean country looked at him and said, "Then, you will have war?" The officer laughed and said, "Of course not." When we have an election it is often hard-fought, and both sides of the political fence are adamant that their candidate is the only hope for the future; but whichever side wins, we all get up the next morning and go about our business. All presidents make mistakes, but they're honorable people.

Yes, there are citizens hurting economically, there are needy families who slip through the cracks in the system, and there are politicians who violate the public trust. There are people who take advantage of their freedoms, who are violent, who are greedy, who are dishonest – unfortunately, this can never be completely eliminated, only battled and reduced. We don't all agree on what is right, and we don't all like some laws or policies. We must do more to protect our environment, and we will have to make sacrifices in order to pay the national debt. Some people have economic woes, and there are improvements we can make in our safety net for the poor, our treatment of the middle class, and how the wealthy are taxed – as well as disagreements about what is needed to improve business and commerce. Education is a thorny issue, with many different opinions on what works best. It's not going to be all fun and games; but then again, it never has been.

The world, and this country, is far from perfect; no one would try to argue that it is. America is a work in progress, and it has been for 226 years. When taken on balance, however, the country doesn't need to come back from anything. The people are still living in the greatest country ever devised, and taken as a whole have a better life than they would anywhere else. There are exceptions – there always are – but our imperfect system beats most others, our imperfect government is more secure than others, our politicians for the most part are trying to do what is right, and those who have the most impact on our lives, ultimately, are still.....well, *us*.

We're not looking for a renaissance, a comeback, a rebirth, or a new direction. We have work to do – we always have – but this isn't halftime of a game that we're losing by two touchdowns. We're still about 21 points ahead and as long as we work harder in the second half, everything is fine.

TOO AMUSING NOT TO SHARE - TAKEN OUTSIDE THE ELKS LODGE:

AND - IRREFUTABLE PROOF OF A SUPREME BEING........

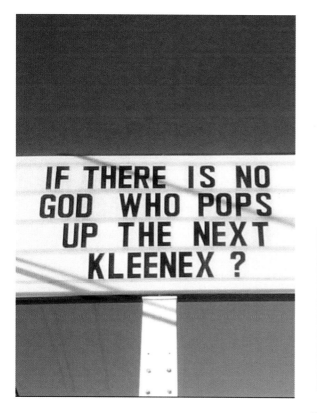

ICE RINKS IN THE COPPER COUNTRY – 1910

Palestra
Laurium

Mohawk

Colosseum
Calumet

CALUMET SUNSET
(until next issue.....)